Mediterranean Cookbook for Whole Family

Quick and Easy Recipes for the Whole Family

Sommario

Introduction

The Mediterranean diet is based on the traditional food that people ate in countries like Greece and Italy. According to research, it has been noted that this diet is much healthier than other types of diets and provides a lower risk of lifestyle diseases.

This obviously applies to people of all ages, it's great for the healthy development of children, for the maintenance of physical fitness of adults, and for the energy it can provide to the elderly.

I created this book to give all families the opportunity to enjoy unique and delicious dishes, but without losing health.

Now get ready in the kitchen and let's start trying these delicious dishes right away.

Breakfast & Brunch Recipes

Almond Pancakes

Servings: 6

Cooking Time: 30 Minutes

Ingredients:

- ½ cup melted coconut oil, plus a little on the side for grease

- 2 cups unsweetened, room temperature almond milk

- 2 teaspoons raw honey

- 1 ½ cups whole wheat flour

- 2 eggs, room temperature

- ¼ teaspoon ground cinnamon

- ½ cup almond flour

- ¼ teaspoon sea salt

- ½ teaspoon baking soda

- 1 ½ teaspoons baking powder

Directions:

1. In a large bowl, whisk your eggs.

2. Add in the coconut oil, honey, and almond milk. Whisk thoroughly.

3. In a separate bowl, sift together your baking soda, baking powder, sea salt, almond flour, cinnamon, and whole wheat flour. Ensure the ingredients are well incorporated.

4. Combine the two mixtures by slowly adding your powdered ingredients into your wet ingredients. Stir as you combine as it will be easier to fully mix the ingredients.

5. Grease a large skillet with oil and set it on medium-high heat.

6. Using ½ cup measurements, pour the batter into the skillet. Make sure the pancakes are not touching each other when they cook.

7. Let your pancakes cook for about 3 to 5 minutes on each side. Once bubbles start to break the surface and the edges become firm, flip the pancake over to cook the other side.

8. Once they are cooked thoroughly, place them on a plate and continue the process until all your batter is used up. You might need to grease your skillet again between batches.

9. To give your pancakes more of a Mediterranean flavor, add some fresh fruit on top.

Nutrition Info: calories: 286, fats: 17 grams, carbohydrates: 26 grams, protein: 7 grams.

Mediterranean Egg Muffins With Ham

Servings: 6

Cooking Time: 15 Minutes

Ingredients:

- 9 Slices of thin cut deli ham

- 1/2 cup canned roasted red pepper, sliced + additional for garnish

- 1/3 cup fresh spinach, minced

- 1/4 cup feta cheese, crumbled

- 5 large eggs

- Pinch of salt

- Pinch of pepper

- 1 1/2 tbsp Pesto sauce

- Fresh basil for garnish

Directions:

1. Preheat oven to 400 degrees F

2. Spray a muffin tin with cooking spray, generously

3. Line each of the muffin tin with 1 ½ pieces of ham - making sure there aren't any holes for the egg mixture come out of

4. Place some of the roasted red pepper in the bottom of each muffin tin

5. Place 1 tbsp of minced spinach on top of each red pepper

6. Top the pepper and spinach off with a large 1/2 tbsp of crumbled feta cheese

7. In a medium bowl, whisk together the eggs salt and pepper, divide the egg mixture evenly among the 6 muffin tins

8. Bake for 15 to 17 minutes until the eggs are puffy and set

9. Remove each cup from the muffin tin

10. Allow to cool completely

11. Distribute the muffins among the containers, store in the fridge for 2 - 3days or in the freezer for 3 months

12. To Serve: Heat in the microwave for 30 seconds or until heated through. Garnish with 1/4 tsp pesto sauce, additional roasted red pepper slices and fresh basil.

Nutrition Info:Per Serving: Calories:109;Carbs: 2g;Total Fat: 6g;Protein: 9g

Overnight Berry Chia Oats

Servings: 1

Cooking Time: 5 Minutes

Ingredients:

- 1/2 cup Quaker Oats rolled oats

- 1/4 cup chia seeds

- 1 cup milk or water

- pinch of salt and cinnamon

- maple syrup, or a different sweetener, to taste

- 1 cup frozen berries of choice or smoothie leftovers

- Toppings:

- Yogurt

- Berries

Directions:

1. In a jar with a lid, add the oats, seeds, milk, salt, and cinnamon, refrigerate overnight

2. On serving day, puree the berries in a blender

3. Stir the oats, add in the berry puree and top with yogurt and more berries, nuts, honey, or garnish of your choice

4. Enjoy!

5. Recipe Notes: Make 3 jars at a time in individual jars for easy grab and go breakfasts for the next few days.

Nutrition Info:Per Serving: Calories:405;Carbs: g;Total Fat: 11g;Protein: 17g

Quinoa

Servings: 4

Cooking Time: 8 Hours

Ingredients:

- 1 cup quinoa (uncooked)

- 2 cups water

- 1 tablespoon raw honey

- 1 cup coconut milk

- Topping(s) of your preference (nuts, cinnamon, etc.)

- sea salt or plain salt

Directions:

1. Start by rinsing the quinoa under running water.

2. Then, add all the Ingredients: in a slow cooker and cover with a lid. Cook the mixture for 8 hours on low.

3. Serve hot with toppings of your choice.

Nutrition Info:Per Serving: Calories: 310, Total Fat: 16.8g, Saturated Fat: 13, Cholesterol: 0 mg, Sodium: 11 mg, Total Carbohydrate: 39 g, Dietary Fiber: 4.3 g, Total Sugars: 6.3 g, Protein: 7.4 g, Vitamin D: 0 mcg, Calcium: 30 mg, Iron: 3 mg, Potassium: 400 mg

Egg, Feta, Spinach, And Artichoke Freezer Breakfast Burritos

Servings: 6

Cooking Time: 5 Minutes

Ingredients:

- 8 large eggs

- ½ teaspoon dried Italian herbs

- ½ teaspoon garlic powder

- ½ teaspoon onion powder

- 3 teaspoons olive oil, divided

- 10 ounces baby spinach leaves

- ½ cup crumbled feta cheese

- 1 (14-ounce) can quartered artichoke hearts, super-tough leaves removed

- 6 (8- or 9-inch) whole-wheat tortillas

- 6 tablespoons prepared hummus or homemade hummus

Directions:

1. Beat the eggs and whisk in the Italian herbs, garlic powder, and onion powder.

2. Heat 1 teaspoon of oil in a 1inch skillet. When the oil is shimmering, add the spinach and sauté for 2 to 3 minutes, until the spinach is wilted. Remove the spinach from the pan.

3. In the same pan, heat the remaining 2 teaspoons of oil. When the oil is hot, add the eggs. When the eggs start to set, stir to scramble. Cook for about minutes, then add the cooked spinach, feta, and artichoke hearts. Cool the mixture and pour off any liquid if it accumulates.

4. Place 1 tortilla on a cutting board. Spread 1 tablespoon of hummus down the middle of the tortilla. Place ¾ cup of the egg filling on top of the hummus. Fold the bottom end and sides over the filling and tightly roll up. Repeat for the remaining 5 tortillas.

5. Wrap each burrito in foil and place in a resealable plastic bag.

6. STORAGE: Store sealed bags in the freezer for up to 3 months. To reheat burritos, unwrap and remove the foil. Cover the burrito with a damp paper towel, place on a microwaveable plate, and microwave on high until the center of the burrito is hot, about 2 minutes.

Nutrition Info:Per Serving: Total calories: 359; Total fat: 18g; Saturated fat: 6g; Sodium: 800mg; Carbohydrates: 32g; Fiber: 6g; Protein: 18g

Breakfast Jalapeno Egg Cups

Servings: 6

Cooking Time: 8 Minutes

Ingredients:

- 12 eggs, lightly beaten

- 1/4 tsp garlic powder

- 1/2 tsp lemon pepper seasoning

- 3 jalapeno peppers, chopped

- 1 cup cheddar cheese, shredded

- Pepper

- Salt

Directions:

1. Pour 1/2 cups of water into the instant pot then place steamer rack in the pot.

2. In a bowl, whisk eggs with lemon pepper seasoning, garlic powder, pepper, and salt.

3. Stir in jalapenos and cheese.

4. Pour mixture between six jars and seal jar with a lid.

5. Place jars on top of the rack in the instant pot.

6. Seal pot with a lid and select manual and set timer for 8 minutes.

7. Once done, allow to release pressure naturally for 10 minutes then release remaining using quick release. Remove lid.

8. Serve and enjoy.

Nutrition Info: Calories: 212;Fat: 15.2 g;Carbohydrates: 3.2 g;Sugar: 2.1 g;Protein: 16.1 g;Cholesterol: 347 mg

Low Carb Waffles

Servings: 2

Cooking Time: 10 Minutes

Ingredients:

- 4 egg whites

- 2 whole eggs

- ½ teaspoon baking powder

- 4 tablespoons milk

- 4 tablespoons coconut flour

- sugar or sweetener to taste

Directions:

1. Whip the egg whites to a stiff peak.

2. When the stiff peaks are attained, add the coconut flour, milk, baking powder, and the whole egg; mix.

3. Start heating your waffle iron to the required temperature. Grease it and pour in the batter. Cook until brown.

4. Serve warm and top with your choice of fruit or other toppings.

Nutrition Info:Per Serving: Calories: 234, Total Fat: 9.1g, Saturated Fat: 7, Cholesterol: 166 mg, Sodium: 204 mg, Total Carbohydrate: 18.9 g, Dietary Fiber: 10 g, Total Sugars: 4.2 g, Protein: 17.7 g, Vitamin D: 16 mcg, Calcium: 118 mg, Iron: 1 mg, Potassium: 310 mg

Potato Breakfast Hash

Servings: 2

Cooking Time: 10 Minutes

Ingredients:

- 1 sweet potato, diced

- 1 cup bell pepper, chopped

- 1 tsp cumin

- 1 tbsp olive oil

- 1 potato, diced

- 1/2 tsp pepper

- 1 tsp paprika

- 1/2 tsp garlic, minced

- 1/4 cup vegetable stock

- 1/2 tsp salt

Directions:

1. Add all ingredients into the instant pot and stir well.

2. Seal pot with lid and cook on high for 10 minutes.

3. Once done, release pressure using quick release. Remove lid.

4. Stir and serve.

Nutrition Info: Calories: 206;Fat: 7.7 g;Carbohydrates: 32.9 g;Sugar: 7.6 g;Protein: 4 g;Cholesterol: 0 mg

Farro Porridge With Blackberry Compote

Servings: 4

Cooking Time: 30 Minutes

Ingredients:

- 1¼ cups uncooked semi-pearled farro

- 5 cups unsweetened vanilla almond milk

- 1 tablespoon pure maple syrup

- 1 (10-ounce) package frozen blackberries (2 cups)

- 2 teaspoons pure maple syrup

- 2 teaspoons balsamic vinegar

Directions:

1. TO MAKE THE FARRO

2. Place the farro, almond milk, and maple syrup in a saucepan. Bring the liquid to a boil, then turn the heat down to low and simmer until the farro is tender and has absorbed much of the liquid, about 30 minutes. It should still look somewhat liquidy and will continue to absorb liquid as it cools.

3. Scoop ¾ cup of farro into each of 4 containers.

4. TO MAKE THE BLACKBERRY COMPOTE

5. While the farro is cooking, place the frozen blackberries, maple syrup, and balsamic vinegar in a separate saucepan on medium-low heat. Cook for 12 to 1minutes, until the blackberry juices have thickened. Cool.

6. Spoon ¼ cup of the blackberry compote into each of the 4 farro containers.

7. STORAGE: Store covered containers in the refrigerator for up to 5 days.

Nutrition Info:Per Serving: Total calories: 334; Total fat: 5g; Saturated fat: 0g; Sodium: 227mg; Carbohydrates: 64g; Fiber: 11g; Protein: 11g

Bulgur Fruit Breakfast Bowl

Servings: 6

Cooking Time: 15 Minutes

Ingredients:

- 2 cups 2% milk

- ½ teaspoon ground cinnamon

- 1 ½ cups bulgur

- ½ cup almonds, chopped

- ½ cup mint, chopped (fresh is preferred)

- 8 dried and chopped figs

- 1 cup water

- 2 cups frozen sweet cherries - you can also substitute in blueberries or blackberries

Directions:

1. Turn your stovetop to medium heat and combine the bulger, water, milk, and cinnamon. Lightly stir as the ingredients come to a boil.

2. Cover your mixture and turn the stove range temperature down to medium-low heat. Let the mixture simmer for 8 to 11 minutes. It is done simmering when about half of the liquid has been absorbed

3. Without removing the pan, turn off the rangetop heat and add the frozen cherries, almonds, and figs. Lightly stir and then cover for one minute so the cherries can thaw, and the mixture can combine.

4. Remove the cover and add in the mint before scooping your breakfast into a bowl.

Nutrition Info: calories: 301, fats: 6 grams, carbohydrates: grams, protein: 9 grams.

Acorn Squash Eggs

Servings: 5

Cooking Time: 30 Minutes

Ingredients:

- 2 acorn squash

- 4 eggs

- 2 tablespoons extra virgin olive oil

- salt

- pepper

- 5-6 dates, pitted

- 8 walnut halves

- bunch fresh parsley

Directions:

1. Preheat oven to 375 degrees F.

2. Cut the squashes crosswise into ¾-inch thick slices; remove seeds.

3. Prepare slices with holes.

4. Line a baking sheet with parchment paper and place the slices on it.

5. Season with salt and pepper and bake for 20 minutes.

6. Chop up walnuts and dates.

7. Remove the baking dish from the oven and drizzle the slices with olive oil.

8. Crack an egg into the center of the slices (into the hole you made) and season with salt and pepper.

9. Sprinkle walnuts on top and put back in the oven for 10 minutes.

10. Add maple syrup.

11. Enjoy!

Nutrition Info:Per Serving: Calories: 198, Total Fat: 9.5g, Saturated Fat: 2, Cholesterol: 131 mg, Sodium: 97 mg, Total Carbohydrate: 25.7 g, Dietary Fiber: 3.9 g, Total Sugars: 5.7 g, Protein: 6.6 g, Vitamin D: mcg, Calcium: 107 mg, Iron: 3 mg, Potassium: 811 mg

Green Smoothie

Servings: 2

Cooking Time: 12 Minutes

Ingredients:

- 4 cups spinach

- 20 almonds, raw

- 2 cups milk

- 2 scoops whey protein

- sweetener of your choice and to taste

Directions:

1. Start by blending spinach, almond, and milk in a blender.

2. Blend until the puree is formed.

3. Add the rest of the Ingredients: and blend well.

4. Pour into glasses and serve.

5. Enjoy.

Nutrition Info:Per Serving: Calories: 325, Total Fat: 13.1 g, Saturated Fat: 4.4 g, Cholesterol: 85 mg, Sodium: 218 mg, Total Carbohydrate: 20.4 g, Dietary Fiber: 2.8 g, Total Sugars: 12.7 g, Protein: 34.4 g, Vitamin D: 1 mcg, Calcium: 482 mg, Iron: 3 mg, Potassium: 738 mg

Lunch and Dinner Recipes

Couscous With Pepperoncini & Tuna

Servings: 4

Cooking Time: 20 Minutes

Ingredients:

- The Couscous:

- Chicken broth or water (1 cup)

- Couscous (1.25 cups)

- Kosher salt (.75 tsp.)

- The Accompaniments:

- Oil-packed tuna (2- 5-oz. cans)

- Cherry tomatoes (1 pint - halved)

- Sliced pepperoncini (.5 cup)

- Chopped fresh parsley (.33 cup)

- Capers (.25 cup)

- Olive oil (for serving)

- Black pepper & kosher salt (as desired)

- Lemon (1 quartered)

Directions:

1. Make the couscous in a small saucepan using water or broth. Prepare it using the medium heat temperature setting. Let it sit for about ten minutes.

2. Toss the tomatoes, tuna, capers, parsley, and pepperoncini into a mixing bowl.

3. Fluff the couscous when done and dust using the pepper and salt. Spritz it using the oil and serve with the tuna mix and a lemon wedge.

Nutrition Info: Calories: 226;Protein: 8 grams;Fat: 1 gram

Tilapia With Avocado & Red Onion

Servings: 4

Cooking Time: 15 Minutes

Ingredients:

- Olive oil (1 tbsp.)

- Sea salt (.25 tsp.)

- Fresh orange juice (1 tbsp.)

- Tilapia fillets (four 4 oz. - more rectangular than square)

- Red onion (.25 cup)

- Sliced avocado (1)

- Also Needed: 9-inch pie plate

Directions:

1. Combine the salt, juice, and oil to add into the pie dish. Work with one fillet at a time. Place it in the dish and turn to coat all sides.

2. Arrange the fillets in a wagon wheel-shaped formation. (Each of the fillets should be in the center of the dish with the other end draped over the edge.

3. Place a tablespoon of the onion on top of each of the fillets and fold the end into the center. Cover the dish with plastic wrap, leaving one corner open to vent the steam.

4. Place in the microwave using the high heat setting for three minutes. It's done when the center can be easily flaked.

5. Top the fillets off with avocado and serve.

Nutrition   Info: Calories: 200;Protein: 22 grams;Fat: 11 grams

Baked Salmon With Dill

Servings: 4

Cooking Time: 15 Minutes

Ingredients:

- Salmon fillets (4- 6 oz. portions - 1-inch thickness)

- Kosher salt (.5 tsp.)

- Finely chopped fresh dill (1.5 tbsp.)

- Black pepper (.125 tsp.)

- Lemon wedges (4)

Directions:

1. Warm the oven in advance to reach 350° Fahrenheit.

2. Lightly grease a baking sheet with a misting of cooking oil spray and add the fish. Lightly

spritz the fish with the spray along with a shake of salt, pepper, and dill.

3. Bake it until the fish is easily flaked (10 min..)

4. Serve with lemon wedges.

Nutrition Info: Calories: 2;Protein: 28 grams;Fat: 16 grams

Steak And Veggies

Servings: 6

Cooking Time: 15 Minutes

Ingredients:

- 2 lbs baby red potatoes

- 16 oz broccoli florets

- 2 tbsp olive oil

- 3 cloves garlic, minced

- 1 tsp dried thyme

- Kosher salt, to taste

- Freshly ground black pepper, to taste

- 2 lbs (1-inch-thick) top sirloin steak, patted dry

Directions:

1. Preheat oven to broil

2. Lightly oil a baking sheet or coat with nonstick spray

3. In a large pot over high heat, boil salted water, cook the potatoes until parboiled for 12-15 minutes, drain well

4. Place the potatoes and broccoli in a single layer onto the prepared baking sheet

5. Add the olive oil, garlic and thyme, season with salt and pepper, to taste and then gently toss to combine

6. Season the steaks with salt and pepper, to taste, and add to the baking sheet in a single layer

7. Place it into oven and broil until the steak is browned and charred at the edges, about 4-5 minutes per side for medium-rare, or until the desired doneness

8. Distribute the steak and veggies among the containers. Store in the fridge for up to 3 days

9. To Serve: Reheat in the microwave for 1-2 minutes. Top with garlic butter and enjoy

Nutrition Info:Per Serving: Calories:460;Total Fat: 24g;Total Carbs: 24g;Fiber: 2.6g;Protein: 37g

Lentil And Roasted Carrot Salad With Herbs And Feta

Servings: 4

Cooking Time: 25 Minutes

Ingredients:

- ¾ cup brown or green lentils

- 3 cups water

- 1 pound baby carrots, halved on the diagonal

- 2 teaspoons olive oil, plus 2 tablespoons

- ½ teaspoon kosher salt, divided

- 1 teaspoon garlic powder

- 1 cup packed parsley leaves, chopped

- ½ cup packed cilantro leaves, chopped

- ¼ cup packed mint leaves, chopped

- ½ teaspoon grated lemon zest

- 4 teaspoons freshly squeezed lemon juice

- ¼ cup crumbled feta cheese

Directions:

1. Preheat the oven to 400°F. Line a sheet pan with a silicone baking mat or parchment paper.

2. Place the lentils and water in a medium saucepan and turn the heat to high. As soon as the water comes to a boil, turn the heat to low and simmer until the lentils are firm yet tender, 10 to minutes (see tip). Drain and cool.

3. While the lentils are cooking, place the carrots on the sheet pan and toss with 2 teaspoons of oil, ¼ teaspoon of salt, and the garlic powder. Roast the carrots in the oven until firm yet tender, about 20 to 25 minutes. Cool when done.

4. In a large bowl, mix the cooled lentils, carrots, parsley, cilantro, mint, lemon zest, lemon juice, feta, the remaining 2 tablespoons of oil, and the remaining ¼ teaspoon of salt. Add more lemon juice and/or salt to taste if needed.

5. Place 1¼ cups of the mixture in each of 4 containers.

6. STORAGE: Store covered containers in the refrigerator for up to 5 days.

Nutrition Info:Per Serving: Total calories: 2; Total fat: 12g; Saturated fat: 3g; Sodium: 492mg; Carbohydrates: 31g; Fiber: 13g; Protein: 12g

Cinnamon Squash Soup

Servings: 6

Cooking Time: 1 Hour

Ingredients:

- 1 small butternut squash, peeled and cut up into 1-inch pieces

- 4 tablespoons extra-virgin olive oil, divided

- 1 small yellow onion

- 2 large garlic cloves

- 1 teaspoon salt, divided

- 1 pinch black pepper

- 1 teaspoon dried oregano

- 2 tablespoons fresh oregano

- 2 cups low sodium chicken stock

- 1 cinnamon stick

- ½ cup canned white kidney beans, drained and rinsed

- 1 small pear, peeled and cored, chopped up into ½ inch pieces

- 2 tablespoons walnut pieces

- ¼ cup Greek yogurt

- 2 tablespoons freshly chopped parsley

Directions:

1. Preheat oven to 425 degrees F.

2. Place squash in bowl and season with a ½ teaspoon of salt and tablespoons of olive oil.

3. Spread the squash onto a roasting pan and roast for about 25 minutes until tender.

4. Set aside squash to let cool.

5. Heat remaining 2 tablespoons of olive oil in a medium-sized pot over medium-high heat.

6. Add onions and sauté until soft.

7. Add dried oregano and garlic and sauté for 1 minute and until fragrant.

8. Add squash, broth, pear, cinnamon stick, pepper, and remaining salt.

9. Bring mixture to a boil.

10. Once the boiling point is reached, add walnuts and beans.

11. Reduce the heat and allow soup to cook for approximately 20 minutes until flavors have blended well.

12. Remove the cinnamon stick.

13. Use an immersion blender and blend the entire mixture until smooth.

14. Add yogurt gradually while whisking to ensure that you are getting a very creamy soup.

15. Season with some additional salt and pepper if needed.

16. Garnish with parsley and fresh oregano.

17. Enjoy!

Nutrition Info:Per Serving: Calories: 197, Total Fat: 11.6 g, Saturated Fat: 1.7 g, Cholesterol: 0 mg, Sodium: 264 mg, Total Carbohydrate: 20.2 g, Dietary Fiber: 7.1 g, Total Sugars: 4.3 g, Protein: 6.1 g, Vitamin D: 0 mcg, Calcium: 103 mg, Iron: 3 mg, Potassium: 425 mg

Creamy Chicken

Servings: 2

Cooking Time: 25 Minutes

Ingredients:

- ½ small onion, chopped

- ¼ cup sour cream

- Salt and black pepper, to taste

- 1 tablespoon butter

- ¼ cup mushrooms

- ½ pound chicken breasts

Directions:

1. Heat butter in a skillet and add onions and mushrooms.

2. Sauté for about 5 minutes and add chicken breasts and salt.

3. Secure the lid and cook for about 5 more minutes.

4. Add sour cream and cook for about 3 minutes.

5. Open the lid and dish out in a bowl to serve immediately.

6. Transfer the creamy chicken breasts in a dish and set aside to cool for meal prepping. Divide them in 2 containers and cover their lid. Refrigerate for 2-3 days and reheat in microwave before serving.

Nutrition Info: Calories: 335 ;Carbohydrates: 2.9g;Protein: 34g;Fat: 20.2g;Sugar: 0.8g;Sodium: 154mg

Chicken Drummies With Peach Glaze

Servings: 4

Cooking Time: 25 Minutes

Ingredients:

- 2 pounds of chicken drummies, remove the skin

- 15 ounce can of sliced peaches, drain the juice

- ¼ cup cider vinegar

- ½ teaspoon paprika

- ¼ teaspoon black pepper

- ¼ cup honey

- 3 garlic cloves

- ¼ teaspoon sea salt

Directions:

1. Before you turn your oven on, make sure that one rack is 4 inches below the broiler element.

2. Set your oven's temperature to 500 degrees Fahrenheit.

3. Line a large baking sheet with a piece of aluminum foil.

4. Set a wire cooling rack on top of the foil.

5. Spray the rack with cooking spray.

6. Add the honey, peaches, garlic, vinegar, salt, paprika, and pepper into a blender. Mix until smooth.

7. Set a medium saucepan on top of your stove and set the range temperature to medium heat.

8. Pour the mixture into the saucepan and bring it to a boil while stirring constantly.

9. Once the sauce is done, divide it into two small bowls and set one off to the side.

10. With the second bowl, brush half of the mixture onto the chicken drummies.

11. Roast the drummies for 10 minutes.

12. Take the drummies out of the oven and switch to broiler mode.

13. Brush the drummies with the other half of the sauce from the second bowl.

14. Again, place the drummies back into the oven and set a timer for 5 minutes.

15. When the timer goes off, flip the drummies over and broil for another 3 to 4 minutes.

16. Serve the drummies with the reserved sauce and enjoy!

Nutrition Info: calories: 291, fats: 5 grams, carbohydrates: 33 grams, protein: 30 grams.

Berry Compote With Orange Mint Infusion

Servings: 8

Cooking Time: 20 Minutes

Ingredients:

- ½ cup water

- 3 orange pekoe tea bags

- 3 sprigs of fresh mint

- 1 cup fresh strawberries, hulled and halved lengthwise

- 1 cup fresh golden raspberries

- 1 cup fresh red raspberries

- 1 cup fresh blueberries

- 1 cup fresh blackberries

- 1 cup fresh sweet cherries, pitted and halved

- 1-milliliter bottle of Sauvignon Blanc

- 2/3 cup sugar

- ½ cup pomegranate juice

- 1 teaspoon vanilla

- fresh mint sprigs

Directions:

1. In a small saucepan, bring water to a boil and add tea bags and 3 mint sprigs.

2. Stir well, cover, remove from heat, and allow to stand for 10 minutes.

3. In a large bowl, add strawberries, red raspberries, golden raspberries, blueberries, blackberries, and cherries. Put to the side.

4. In a medium-sized saucepan, and add the wine, sugar, and pomegranate juice.

5. Pour the infusion (tea mixture) through a fine-mesh sieve and into the pan with wine.

6. Squeeze the bags to release the liquid, and then discard bags and mint springs.

7. Cook well until the sugar has completely dissolved; remove from heat.

8. Stir in vanilla and allow to chill for 2 hours.

9. Pour the mix over the fruits.

10. Garnish with mint sprigs and serve.

11. Enjoy!

Nutrition Info:Per Serving: Calories: 119, Total Fat: 0.3 g, Saturated Fat: 0 g, Cholesterol: 0 mg, Sodium: 3 mg, Total Carbohydrate: 31.6 g, Dietary Fiber: 5 g, Total Sugars: 26.2 g, Protein: 1.2 g, Vitamin D: 0 mcg, Calcium: 28 mg, Iron: 1 mg, Potassium: 158 mg

Quinoa Bruschetta Salad

Servings: 5

Cooking Time: 15 Minutes

Ingredients:

- 2 cups water

- 1 cup uncooked quinoa

- 1 (10-ounce) container cherry tomatoes, quartered

- 1 teaspoon chopped garlic

- 1¼ cups thinly sliced scallions, white and green parts (1 small bunch)

- 1 (8-ounce) container fresh whole-milk mozzarella balls (ciliegine), quartered

- 2 tablespoons balsamic vinegar

- 2 tablespoons olive oil

- ½ teaspoon kosher salt

- ½ cup fresh basil leaves, chiffonaded (cut into strips)

Directions:

1. Place the water and quinoa in a saucepan and bring to a boil. Cover, turn the heat to low, and simmer for minutes.

2. While the quinoa is cooking, place the tomatoes, garlic, scallions, mozzarella, vinegar, and oil in a large mixing bowl. Stir to combine.

3. Once the quinoa is cool, add it to the tomato mixture along with the salt and basil. Mix to combine.

4. Place 1⅓ cups of the mixture in each of 5 containers and refrigerate. Serve at room temperature.

5. STORAGE: Store covered containers in the refrigerator for up to days.

Nutrition Info:Per Serving: Total calories: 323; Total fat: 1; Saturated fat: 6g; Sodium: 317mg; Carbohydrates: 30g; Fiber: 4g; Protein: 14g

Zesty Lemon Parmesan Chicken And Zucchini Noodles

Servings: 2

Cooking Time: 15 Minutes

Ingredients:

- 2 packages Frozen zucchini noodle Spirals

- 1-1/2 lbs. boneless skinless chicken breast, cut into bite-sized pieces

- 1 tsp fine sea salt

- 2 tsp dried oregano

- 1/2 tsp ground black pepper

- 4 garlic cloves, minced

- 2 tbsp vegan butter

- 2 tsp lemon zest

- 2 tsp oil

- 1/3 cup parmesan

- 2/3 cup broth

- Lemon slices, for garnish

- Parsley, for garnish

Directions:

1. Cook zucchini noodles according to package instructions, drain well

2. In a large skillet over medium heat, add the oil

3. Season chicken with salt and pepper, brown chicken pieces, for about 4 minutes per side depending on the thickness, or until cooked through – Work in cook in batches if necessary

4. Transfer the chicken to a pan

5. In the same skillet, add in the garlic, and cook until fragrant about 30 seconds

6. Add in the butter, oregano and lemon zest, pour in chicken broth to deglaze making sure to scrape up all the browned bits stuck to the bottom of the pan

7. Turn the heat up to medium-high, bring sauce and chicken up to a boil, immediately lower the heat and stir in the parmesan cheese

8. Place the chicken back in pan and allow it to gently simmer for 3-4 minutes, or until sauce has slightly reduced and thickened up

9. Taste and adjust seasoning, allow the noodles to cool completely

10. Distribute among the containers, store for 2-3 days

11. To Serve: Reheat in the microwave for 1-2 minutes or until heated through. Garnish with the fresh parsley and lemon slices and enjoy!

Nutrition Info:Per Serving: Calories:633;Carbs: 4g;Total Fat: 35g;Protein: 70g

Three Citrus Sauce Scallops

Servings: 4

Cooking Time: 15 Minutes

Ingredients:

- 2 teaspoons extra virgin olive oil

- 1 shallot, minced

- 20 sea scallops, cleaned

- 1 tablespoon lemon zest

- 2 teaspoons orange zest

- 1 teaspoon lime zest

- 1 tablespoon fresh basil, chopped

- ½ cup freshly squeezed lemon juice

- 2 tablespoons honey

- 1 tablespoon plain Greek yogurt

- Pinch of sea salt

Directions:

1. Take a large skillet and place it over medium-high heat

2. Add olive oil and heat it up

3. Add shallots and Saute for 1 minute

4. Add scallops in the skillet and sear for 5 minutes, turning once

5. Move scallops to edge and stir in lemon, orange, lime zest, basil, orange juice and lemon juice

6. Simmer the sauce for 3 minutes

7. Whisk in honey, yogurt and salt

8. Cook for 4 minutes and coat the scallops in the sauce

9. Serve and enjoy!

10. Meal Prep/Storage Options: Store in airtight containers in your fridge for 1-2 days.

Nutrition Info: Calories: 207;Fat: 4g;Carbohydrates: 17g;Protein: 26g

Steamed Mussels Topped With Wine Sauce

Servings: 4

Cooking Time: 15 Minutes

Ingredients:

- 2 pounds mussels

- 1 tablespoon extra virgin olive oil

- 1 cup sliced onion

- 1 cup dry white wine

- ¼ teaspoon ground black pepper

- ¼ teaspoon sea salt

- 3 sliced cloves of garlic

- 2 lemon slices

- Optional: lemon wedges for serving

Directions:

1. Set a large colander in the sink and turn your water to cold.

2. Run water over the mussels, but do not let them sit in the water. If you notice any shells that are not tightly sealed or are cracked, you need to discard them. All shells need to be closed tightly.

3. Turn off the water and leave the mussels in the colander.

4. Set a large skillet on your stovetop and turn your range heat to medium-high.

5. Pour the olive oil into the skillet and allow it to heat up before you add the onion.

6. Saute the onion for 2 to 3 minutes.

7. Combine the garlic and cook the mixture for another minute while stirring continuously.

8. Pour in the wine, pepper, lemon slices, and salt. Stir the ingredients as you bring them to a boil.

9. Add the mussels and place the lid on the skillet.

10. Cook the mixture for 3 to 4 minutes or until the shells begin to open on the mussels. It will help to gently pick up the skillet and shake it a couple of times when the mussels are cooking.

11. If you notice any shells that did not open, use a spoon and discard them.

12. Scoop the mussels into a serving bowl and pour the mixture over the top.

13. If you have lemon wedges, place them on the top of the steamed mussels before serving. Enjoy!

Nutrition Info: calories: 222, fats: 7 grams, carbohydrates: 11 grams, protein: 18 grams.

Spice Potato Soup

Servings: 4-6

Cooking Time: 30 Minutes

Ingredients:

- 2 tablespoons extra virgin olive oil

- 1 large onion, chopped

- 2 garlic cloves, crushed

- 1 pound sweet potatoes, peeled and cut into medium pieces

- ½ teaspoon ground cumin

- ¼ teaspoon ground chili

- ½ teaspoon ground coriander

- ¼ teaspoon ground cinnamon

- ¼ teaspoon salt

- 2 cups chicken stock

- ¼ cup of low-fat crème Fraiche

- 2 tablespoons freshly chopped parsley

- coriander

Directions:

1. Heat olive oil in a large pan over medium-high heat.

2. Add onions and sauté until slightly browned.

3. Reduce heat to medium, add garlic, and keep cooking for 2-minutes more.

4. Add sweet potatoes and sauté for 3-minutes.

5. Add the remaining spices and season with salt.

6. Cook for 2 minutes.

7. Add stock, turn the heat up, and bring the mixture to a boil, stirring occasionally.

8. Cover and lower heat to a slow simmer.

9. Cook for 20 minutes until the potatoes are tender.

10. Remove the pan from the heat.

11. Take an immersion blender and puree the whole mixture.

12. Add a bit of water if the soup is too thick.

13. Check the soup for seasoning.

14. Ladle the soup into your jars.

15. Give a swirl of crème Fraiche.

16. Sprinkle with chopped parsley.

17. Enjoy!

Nutrition Info:Per Serving: Calories: 176, Total Fat: 8.4 g, Saturated Fat: 0.8 g, Cholesterol: 0 mg, Sodium: 362 mg, Total Carbohydrate: 24.3 g, Dietary Fiber: 3.8 g, Total Sugars: 1.7 g, Protein: 2 g, Vitamin D: 0 mcg, Calcium: 30 mg, Iron: 1 mg, Potassium: 675 mg

Spicy Cajun Shrimp

Servings: 2

Cooking Time: 50 Minutes

Ingredients:

- 3 cloves garlic, crushed

- 4 tablespoons butter, divided

- 2 large zucchini, spiraled

- 1 red pepper, sliced

- 1 onion, sliced

- 20-30 jumbo shrimp

- 1 teaspoon paprika

- dash cayenne pepper

- ½ teaspoon of sea salt

- dash red pepper flakes

- 1 teaspoon garlic powder

- 1 teaspoon onion powder

Directions:

1. Pass the zucchini through a spiralizer.

2. Combine the Ingredients: listed under Cajun Seasoning above.

3. Add oil and 2 tablespoons of butter to a pan and allow to heat up over medium heat.

4. Add onion and red pepper and sauté for minutes.

5. Add shrimp and cook well.

6. Place the remaining 2 tablespoons of butter in another pan and allow it to melt over medium heat.

7. Add zucchini noodles and sauté for 3 minutes.

8. Transfer the noodles to a container.

9. Top with the prepared Cajun shrimp and veggie mix.

10. Season with salt and enjoy!

Nutrition Info:Per Serving: Calories: 734, Total Fat: 24.2 g, Saturated Fat: 14.7 g, Cholesterol: 12mg, Sodium: 6703 mg, Total Carbohydrate: 29.1 g, Dietary Fiber: 7.1 g, Total Sugars: 24.9 g, Protein: 106.8 g, Vitamin D: 16 mcg, Calcium: 694 mg, Iron: 6 mg, Potassium: 1229 mg

Pan-seared Salmon

Servings: 4

Cooking Time: 20 Minutes

Ingredients:

- Salmon fillets (4 @ 6 oz. each)

- Olive oil (2 tbsp.)

- Capers (2 tbsp.)

- Pepper & salt (.125 tsp. each)

- Lemon (4 slices)

Directions:

1. Warm a heavy skillet for about three minutes using the medium heat temperature setting.

2. Lightly spritz the salmon with oil. Arrange them in the pan and increase the temperature setting to high.

3. Sear for approximately three minutes. Sprinkle with the salt, pepper, and capers.

4. Flip the salmon over and continue cooking for five minutes or until browned the way you like it.

5. Garnish with lemon slices and serve.

Nutrition Info: Calories: 371;Protein: 33.7 grams;Fat: 25.1 grams

Pasta Faggioli Soup

Servings: 8

Cooking Time: 1 Hour

Ingredients:

- 1 28-ounce can diced tomatoes

- 1 14-ounce can great northern beans, undrained

- 14 ounces spinach, chopped and drained

- 1 14-ounce can tomato sauce

- 3 cups chicken broth

- 1 tablespoon garlic, minced

- 8 slices bacon, cooked crisp, crumbled

- 1 tablespoon dried parsley

- 1 teaspoon garlic powder

- 1½ teaspoons salt

- ½ teaspoon ground black pepper

- ½ teaspoon dried basil

- ½ pound seashell pasta

- 3 cups water

Directions:

1. Take a large stockpot and add the diced tomatoes, spinach, beans, chicken broth, tomato sauce, water, bacon, garlic, parsley, garlic powder, pepper, salt, and basil.

2. Put it over medium-high heat and bring the mixture to a boil.

3. Immediately reduce the heat to low and simmer for 40 minutes, covered.

4. Add pasta and cook uncovered for about 10 minutes until al dente.

5. Ladle the soup into serving bowls.

6. Sprinkle some cheese on top.

7. Enjoy!

Nutrition Info:Per Serving: Calories: 23 Total Fat: 2.3 g, Saturated Fat: 0.7 g, Cholesterol: 2 mg, Sodium: 2232 mg, Total Carbohydrate: 40.6 g, Dietary Fiber: 13.1 g, Total Sugars: 6.4 g, Protein: 16.3 g, Vitamin D: 0 mcg, Calcium: 160 mg, Iron: 5 mg, Potassium: 1455 mg

Fattoush Salad

Servings: 4

Cooking Time: 10 Minutes

Ingredients:

- 2 loaves pita bread

- 3 tablespoons extra virgin olive oil

- ½ teaspoon of sumac

- salt

- pepper

- 1 heart romaine lettuce, chopped

- 1 English cucumber, chopped

- 5 Roma tomatoes, chopped

- 5 green onions, chopped

- 5 radishes, stems removed, thinly sliced

- 2 cups fresh parsley leaves, stems removed, chopped

- 1 cup fresh mint leaves, chopped

- lime juice, 1½ limes

- 1/3 bottle extra virgin olive oil

- salt

- pepper

- 1 teaspoon ground sumac

- ¼ teaspoon ground cinnamon

- scant ¼ teaspoon ground allspice

Directions:

1. Toast pita bread until crisp but not browned.

2. Heat 3 tablespoons of olive oil in a large pan over medium heat.

3. Break the toasted pita into pieces and add them to the oil.

4. Fry pita bread until browned, making sure to toss them from time to time.

5. Add salt, ½ a teaspoon of sumac, and pepper.

6. Remove the pita from the heat and place on a paper towel to drain.

7. In a large mixing bowl, combine lettuce, tomatoes, cucumber, green onions, parsley, and radish.

8. Before serving, make the lime vinaigrette by mixing all Ingredients: listed above under vinaigrette in a separate bowl.

9. Pour the vinaigrette over the Ingredients: in the other bowl and gently toss.

10. Add pita chips on top and the remaining sumac.

11. Give it a final toss and enjoy!

Nutrition Info:Per Serving: Calories: 200, Total Fat: 11.5 g, Saturated Fat: 1.7 g, Cholesterol: 0 mg, Sodium: 113 mg, Total Carbohydrate: 23.5 g, Dietary Fiber: 5.8 g, Total Sugars: 6.6 g, Protein: 5.2 g, Vitamin D: 0 mcg, Calcium: 145 mg, Iron: 6 mg, Potassium: 852 mg

Sauces and Dressings Recipes

North African Spiced Sautéed Cabbage

Servings: 4

Cooking Time: 10 Minutes

Ingredients:

- 2 teaspoons olive oil

- 1 small head green cabbage (about 1½ to 2 pounds), cored and thinly sliced

- 1 teaspoon ground coriander

- 1 teaspoon garlic powder

- ½ teaspoon caraway seeds

- ½ teaspoon ground cumin

- ¼ teaspoon kosher salt

- Pinch red chili flakes (optional—if you don't like heat, omit it)

- 1 teaspoon freshly squeezed lemon juice

Directions:

1. Heat the oil in a -inch skillet over medium-high heat. Once the oil is hot, add the cabbage and cook down for 3 minutes. Add the coriander, garlic powder, caraway seeds, cumin, salt, and chili flakes (if using) and stir to combine. Continue cooking the cabbage for about 7 more minutes.

2. Stir in the lemon juice and cool.

3. Place 1 heaping cup of cabbage in each of 4 containers.

4. STORAGE: Store covered containers in the refrigerator for up to 5 days.

Nutrition Info:Per Serving: Total calories: 69; Total fat: 3g; Saturated fat: <1g; Sodium: 178mg; Carbohydrates: 11g; Fiber: 4g; Protein: 3g

Blueberry, Flax, And Sunflower Butter Bites

Servings: 6

Cooking Time: 10 Minutes

Ingredients:

- ¼ cup ground flaxseed

- ½ cup unsweetened sunflower butter, preferably unsalted

- ⅓ cup dried blueberries

- 2 tablespoons all-fruit blueberry preserves

- Zest of 1 lemon

- 2 tablespoons unsalted sunflower seeds

- ⅓ cup rolled oats

Directions:

1. Mix all the ingredients in a medium mixing bowl until well combined.

2. Form 1balls, slightly smaller than a golf ball, from the mixture and place on a plate in the freezer for about 20 minutes to firm up.

3. Place 2 bites in each of 6 containers and refrigerate.

4. STORAGE: Store covered containers in the refrigerator for up to 5 days. Bites may also be stored in the freezer for up to 3 months.

Nutrition Info:Per Serving: Total calories: 229; Total fat: 14g; Saturated fat: 1g; Sodium: 1mg; Carbohydrates: 26g; Fiber: 3g; Protein: 7g

Dijon Red Wine Vinaigrette

Servings: ½ Cup

Cooking Time: 5 Minutes

Ingredients:

- 2 teaspoons Dijon mustard

- 3 tablespoons red wine vinegar

- 1 tablespoon water

- ¼ teaspoon dried oregano

- ¼ teaspoon chopped garlic

- ⅛ teaspoon kosher salt

- ¼ cup olive oil

Directions:

1. Place the mustard, vinegar, water, oregano, garlic, and salt in a small bowl and whisk to combine.

2. Whisk in the oil, pouring it into the mustard-vinegar mixture in a thin steam.

3. Pour the vinaigrette into a container and refrigerate.

4. STORAGE: Store the covered container in the refrigerator for up to 2 weeks. Allow the vinaigrette to come to room temperature and shake before serving.

5. Nutrition Info:Per Serving (2 tablespoons): Total calories: 123; Total fat: 14g; Saturated fat: 2g; Sodium: 133mg; Carbohydrates: 0g; Fiber: 0g; Protein: 0g

Hummus

Servings: 1½ Cups

Cooking Time: 5 Minutes

Ingredients:

- 1 (15-ounce) can low-sodium chickpeas, drained and rinsed

- ¼ cup unsalted tahini

- ½ teaspoon chopped garlic

- ¼ cup freshly squeezed lemon juice

- ¼ teaspoon kosher salt

- 3 tablespoons olive oil

- 3 tablespoons cold water

Directions:

1. Place all the ingredients in a food processor or blender and blend until smooth.

2. Taste and adjust the seasonings if needed.

3. Scoop the hummus into a container and refrigerate.

4. STORAGE: Store the covered container in the refrigerator for up to 5 days.

5. Nutrition Info:Per Serving (¼ cup): Total calories: 192; Total fat: 13g; Saturated fat: 2g; Sodium: 109mg; Carbohydrates: 16g; Fiber: ; Protein: 5g

Candied Walnuts

Maple-cinnamon

Servings: 4

Cooking Time: 15 Minutes

Ingredients:

- 1 cup walnut halves

- ½ teaspoon ground cinnamon

- 2 tablespoons pure maple syrup

Directions:

1. Preheat the oven to 325°F. Line a baking sheet with a silicone baking mat or parchment paper.

2. In a small bowl, mix the walnuts, cinnamon, and maple syrup until the walnuts are coated.

3. Pour the nuts onto the baking sheet, making sure to scrape out all the maple syrup. Bake for 15 minutes. Allow the nuts to cool completely.

4. Place ¼ cup of nuts in each of containers or resealable sandwich bags.

5. STORAGE: Store covered containers at room temperature for up to 7 days.

Nutrition Info:Per Serving: Total calories: 190; Total fat: 17g; Saturated fat: 2g; Sodium: 2mg; Carbohydrates: 10g; Fiber: 2g; Protein: 4g

Soups and Salads Recipes

Split Pea Soup

Servings: 6

Cooking Time: 30 Minutes

Ingredients:

- 3 tablespoons butter

- 1 onion diced

- 2 ribs celery diced

- 2 carrots diced

- 6 oz. diced ham

- 1 lb. dry split peas sorted and rinsed

- 6 cups chicken stock

- 2 bay leaves

- kosher salt and black pepper

Directions:

1. Set your Instant Pot on Sauté mode and melt butter in it.

2. Stir in celery, onion, carrots, salt, and pepper.

3. Sauté them for 5 minutes then stir in split peas, ham bone, chicken stock, and bay leaves.

4. Seal and lock the Instant Pot lid then select Manual mode for 15 minutes at high pressure.

5. Once done, release the pressure completely then remove the lid.

6. Remove the ham bone and separate meat from the bone.

7. Shred or dice the meat and return it to the soup.

8. Adjust seasoning as needed then serve warm.

9. Enjoy.

Nutrition   Info: Calories: 190;Carbohydrate: 30.5g;Protein: 8g;Fat: 3.5g;Sugar: 4.2g;Sodium: 461mg

Butternut Squash Soup

Servings: 4

Cooking Time: 40 Minutes

Ingredients:

- 1 tablespoon olive oil

- 1 medium yellow onion chopped

- 1 large carrot chopped

- 1 celery rib chopped

- 3 cloves of garlic minced

- 2 lbs. butternut squash, peeled chopped

- 2 cups vegetable broth

- 1 green apple peeled, cored, and chopped

- 1/4 teaspoon ground cinnamon

- 1 sprig fresh thyme

- 1 sprig fresh rosemary

- 1 teaspoon kosher salt

- 1/2 teaspoon black pepper

- Pinch of nutmeg optional

Directions:

1. Preheat olive oil in the insert of the Instant Pot on Sauté mode.

2. Add celery, carrots, and garlic, sauté for 5 minutes.

3. Stir in squash, broth, cinnamon, apple nutmeg, rosemary, thyme, salt, and pepper.

4. Mix well gently then seal and secure the lid.

5. Select Manual mode to cook for 10 minutes at high pressure.

6. Once done, release the pressure completely then remove the lid.

7. Puree the soup using an immersion blender.

8. Serve warm.

Nutrition Info: Calories: 282;Carbohydrate: 50g;Protein: 13g;Fat: 4.7g;Sugar: 12.8g;Sodium: 213mg

Desserts Recipes

Peaches With Blue Cheese Cream

Servings: 4

Cooking Time: 20 Hours 10 Minutes

Ingredients:

- 4 peaches

- 1 cinnamon stick

- 4 ounces sliced blue cheese

- ⅓ cup orange juice, freshly squeezed is best

- 3 whole cloves

- 1 teaspoon of orange zest, taken from the orange peel

- ¼ teaspoon cardamom pods

- ⅔ cup red wine

- 2 tablespoons honey, raw or your preferred variety

- 1 vanilla bean

- 1 teaspoon allspice berries

- 4 tablespoons dried cherries

Directions:

1. Set a saucepan on top of your stove range and add the cinnamon stick, cloves, orange juice, cardamom, vanilla, allspice, red wine, and orange zest. Whisk the ingredients well.

2. Add your peaches to the mixture and poach them for hours or until they become soft.

3. Take a spoon to remove the peaches and boil the rest of the liquid to make the syrup. You want the liquid to reduce itself by at least half.

4. While the liquid is boiling, combine the dried cherries, blue cheese, and honey into a bowl.

5. Once your peaches are cooled, slice them into halves.

6. Top each peach with the blue cheese mixture and then drizzle the liquid onto the top.

7. Serve and enjoy!

Nutrition Info: calories: 211, fats: 24 grams, carbohydrates: 15 grams, protein: 6 grams.

Stuffed Figs

Servings: 6

Cooking Time: 20 Minutes

Ingredients:

- 10 halved fresh figs

- 20 chopped almonds

- 4 ounces goat cheese, divided

- 2 tablespoons of raw honey

Directions:

1. Turn your oven to broiler mode and set it to a high temperature.

2. Place your figs, cut side up, on a baking sheet. If you like to place a piece of parchment paper on top you can do this, but it is not necessary.

3. Sprinkle each fig with half of the goat cheese.

4. Add a tablespoon of chopped almonds to each fig.

5. Broil the figs for 3 to 4 minutes.

6. Take them out of the oven and let them cool for 5 to 7 minutes.

7. Sprinkle with the remaining goat cheese and honey.

Nutrition Info: calories: 209, fats: 9 grams, carbohydrates: 26 grams, protein: grams.

Chia Pudding With Strawberries

Servings: 4

Cooking Time: 4 Hours 5 Minutes

Ingredients:

- 2 cups unsweetened almond milk

- 1 tablespoon vanilla extract

- 2 tablespoons raw honey

- ¼ cup chia seeds

- 2 cups fresh and sliced strawberries

Directions:

1. In a medium bowl, combine the honey, chia seeds, vanilla, and unsweetened almond milk. Mix well.

2. Set the mixture in the refrigerator for at least 4 hours.

3. When you serve the pudding, top it with strawberries. You can even create a design in a glass serving bowl or dessert dish by adding a little pudding on the bottom, a few strawberries, top the strawberries with some more pudding, and then top the dish with a few strawberries.

Nutrition Info: calories: 108, fats: grams, carbohydrates: 17 grams, protein: 3 grams.

Meat Recipes

Oven-roasted Spare Ribs

Servings: 6

Cooking Time: 3 Hour 40 Minutes

Ingredients:

- 2 pounds spare ribs

- 1 garlic clove, minced

- 1 teaspoon dried marjoram

- 1 lime, halved

- Salt and ground black pepper, to taste

Directions:

1. Toss all ingredients in a ceramic dish.

2. Cover and let it refrigerate for 5 to 6 hours.

3. Roast the foil-wrapped ribs in the preheated oven at 275 degrees F degrees for about hours 30 minutes.

4. Storing

5. Divide the ribs into six portions. Place each portion of ribs in an airtight container; keep in your refrigerator for 3 to days.

6. For freezing, place the ribs in airtight containers or heavy-duty freezer bags. Freeze up to 4 to months. Defrost in the refrigerator and reheat in the preheated oven. Bon appétit!

Nutrition Info: 385 Calories; 29g Fat; 1.8g Carbs; 28.3g Protein; 0.1g Fiber

Parmesan Chicken Salad

Servings: 6

Cooking Time: 20 Minutes

Ingredients:

- 2 romaine hearts, leaves separated

- Flaky sea salt and ground black pepper, to taste

- 1/4 teaspoon chili pepper flakes

- 1 teaspoon dried basil

- 1/4 cup Parmesan, finely grated

- 2 chicken breasts

- 2 Lebanese cucumbers, sliced

- For the dressing:

- 2 large egg yolks

- 1 teaspoon Dijon mustard

- 1 tablespoon fresh lemon juice

- 1/4 cup olive oil

- 2 garlic cloves, minced

Directions:

1. In a grilling pan, cook the chicken breast until no longer pink or until a meat thermometer registers 5 degrees F. Slice the chicken into strips.

2. Storing

3. Place the chicken breasts in airtight containers or Ziploc bags; keep in your refrigerator for to 4 days.

4. For freezing, place the chicken breasts in airtight containers or heavy-duty freezer bags. It will maintain the best quality for about months. Defrost in the refrigerator.

5. Toss the chicken with the other ingredients. Prepare the dressing by whisking all the ingredients.

6. Dress the salad and enjoy! Keep the salad in your refrigerator for 3 to 5 days.

Nutrition Info: 183 Calories; 12.5g Fat; 1. Carbs; 16.3g Protein; 0.9g Fiber

Turkey Wings With Gravy

Servings: 6

Cooking Time: 6 Hours

Ingredients:

- 2 pounds turkey wings

- 1/2 teaspoon cayenne pepper

- 4 garlic cloves, sliced

- 1 large onion, chopped

- Salt and pepper, to taste

- 1 teaspoon dried marjoram

- 1 tablespoon butter, room temperature

- 1 tablespoon Dijon mustard

- For the Gravy:

- 1 cup double cream

- Salt and black pepper, to taste

- 1/2 stick butter

- 3/4 teaspoon guar gum

Directions:

1. Rub the turkey wings with the Dijon mustard and tablespoon of butter. Preheat a grill pan over medium-high heat.

2. Sear the turkey wings for 10 minutes on all sides.

3. Transfer the turkey to your Crock pot; add in the garlic, onion, salt, pepper, marjoram, and cayenne pepper. Cover and cook on low setting for 6 hours.

4. Melt 1/2 stick of the butter in a frying pan. Add in the cream and whisk until cooked through.

5. Next, stir in the guar gum, salt, and black pepper along with cooking juices. Let it cook until the sauce has reduced by half.

6. Storing

7. Wrap the turkey wings in foil before packing them into airtight containers; keep in your refrigerator for up to 3 to 4 days.

8. For freezing, place the turkey wings in airtight containers or heavy-duty freezer bags. Freeze up to 2 to 3 months. Defrost in the refrigerator.

9. Keep your gravy in refrigerator for up to 2 days.

Nutrition Info: 280 Calories; 22.2g Fat; 4.3g Carbs; 15.8g Protein; 0.8g Fiber

Pork Chops With Herbs

Servings: 4

Cooking Time: 20 Minutes

Ingredients:

- 1 tablespoon butter

- 1 pound pork chops

- 2 rosemary sprigs, minced

- 1 teaspoon dried marjoram

- 1 teaspoon dried parsley

- A bunch of spring onions, roughly chopped

- 1 thyme sprig, minced

- 1/2 teaspoon granulated garlic

- 1/2 teaspoon paprika, crushed

- Coarse salt and ground black pepper, to taste

Directions:

1. Season the pork chops with the granulated garlic, paprika, salt, and black pepper.

2. Melt the butter in a frying pan over a moderate flame. Cook the pork chops for 6 to 8 minutes, turning them occasionally to ensure even cooking.

3. Add in the remaining ingredients and cook an additional 4 minutes.

4. Storing

5. Divide the pork chops into four portions; place each portion in a separate airtight container or Ziploc bag; keep in your refrigerator for 3 to 4 days.

6. Freeze the pork chops in airtight containers or heavy-duty freezer bags. Freeze up to 4 months. Defrost in the refrigerator. Bon appétit!

Nutrition Info: 192 Calories; 6.9g Fat; 0.9g Carbs; 29.8g Protein; 0.4g Fiber

Ground Pork Stuffed Peppers

Servings: 4

Cooking Time: 40 Minutes

Ingredients:

- 6 bell peppers, deveined

- 1 tablespoon vegetable oil

- 1 shallot, chopped

- 1 garlic clove, minced

- 1/2 pound ground pork

- 1/3 pound ground veal

- 1 ripe tomato, chopped

- 1/2 teaspoon mustard seeds

- Sea salt and ground black pepper, to taste

Directions:

1. Parboil the peppers for 5 minutes.

2. Heat the vegetable oil in a frying pan that is preheated over a moderate heat. Cook the shallot and garlic for 3 to 4 minutes until they've softened.

3. Stir in the ground meat and cook, breaking apart with a fork, for about 6 minutes. Add the chopped tomatoes, mustard seeds, salt, and pepper.

4. Continue to cook for 5 minutes or until heated through. Divide the filling between the peppers and transfer them to a baking pan.

5. Bake in the preheated oven at 36degrees F approximately 25 minutes.

6. Storing

7. Place the peppers in airtight containers or Ziploc bags; keep in your refrigerator for up to 3 to 4 days.

8. For freezing, place the peppers in airtight containers or heavy-duty freezer bags. Freeze up to 2 to 3 months. Defrost in the refrigerator. Bon appétit!

Nutrition Info: 2 Calories; 20.5g Fat; 8.2g Carbs; 18.2g Protein; 1.5g Fiber

Sides & Appetizers Recipes

Basil Pasta

Servings: 4

Cooking Time: 40 Minutes

Ingredients:

- 2 red peppers, de-seeded and cut into chunks

- 2 red onions cut into wedges

- 2 mild red chilies, de-seeded and diced

- 3 garlic cloves, coarsely chopped

- 1 teaspoon golden caster sugar

- 2 tablespoons olive oil, plus extra for serving

- 2 pounds small ripe tomatoes, quartered

- 12 ounces pasta

- a handful of basil leaves, torn

- 2 tablespoons grated parmesan

- salt

- pepper

Directions:

1. Preheat oven to 390 degrees F.

2. On a large roasting pan, spread peppers, red onion, garlic, and chilies.

3. Sprinkle sugar on top.

4. Drizzle olive oil and season with salt and pepper.

5. Roast the veggies for 1minutes.

6. Add tomatoes and roast for another 15 minutes.

7. In a large pot, cook your pasta in salted boiling water according to instructions.

8. Once ready, drain pasta.

9. Remove the veggies from the oven and carefully add pasta.

10. Toss everything well and let it cool.

11. Spread over the containers.

12. Before eating, place torn basil leaves on top, and sprinkle with parmesan.

13. Enjoy!

Nutrition Info:Per Serving: Calories: 384, Total Fat: 10.8 g, Saturated Fat: 2.3 g, Cholesterol: 67 mg, Sodium: 133 mg, Total Carbohydrate: 59.4 g, Dietary Fiber: 2.3 g, Total Sugars: 5.7 g, Protein: 1 g, Vitamin D: 0 mcg, Calcium: 105 mg, Iron: 4 mg, Potassium: 422 mg

Red Onion Kale Pasta

Servings: 4

Cooking Time: 25 Minutes

Ingredients:

- 2½ cups vegetable broth

- ¾ cup dry lentils

- ½ teaspoon of salt

- 1 bay leaf

- ¼ cup olive oil

- 1 large red onion, chopped

- 1 teaspoon fresh thyme, chopped

- ½ teaspoon fresh oregano, chopped

- 1 teaspoon salt, divided

- ½ teaspoon black pepper

- 8 ounces vegan sausage, sliced into ¼-inch slices

- 1 bunch kale, stems removed and coarsely chopped

- 1 pack rotini

Directions:

1. Add vegetable broth, ½ teaspoons of salt, bay leaf, and lentils to a saucepan over high heat and bring to a boil.

2. Reduce the heat to medium-low and allow to cook for about minutes until tender.

3. Discard the bay leaf.

4. Take another skillet and heat olive oil over medium-high heat.

5. Stir in thyme, onions, oregano, ½ a teaspoon of salt, and pepper; cook for 1 minute.

6. Add sausage and reduce heat to medium-low.

7. Cook for 10 minutes until the onions are tender.

8. Bring water to a boil in a large pot, and then add rotini pasta and kale.

9. Cook for about 8 minutes until al dente.

10. Remove a bit of the cooking water and put it to the side.

11. Drain the pasta and kale and return to the pot.

12. Stir in both the lentils mixture and the onions mixture.

13. Add the reserved cooking liquid to add just a bit of moistness.

14. Spread over containers.

Nutrition Info:Per Serving: Calories: 508, Total Fat: 17 g, Saturated Fat: 3 g, Cholesterol: 0 mg,

Sodium: 2431 mg, Total Carbohydrate: 59.3 g, Dietary Fiber: 6 g, Total Sugars: 4.8 g, Protein: 30.9 g, Vitamin D: 0 mcg, Calcium: 256 mg, Iron: 8 mg, Potassium: 1686 mg

Great Mediterranean Diet Recipes

Popcorn Trail Mix

Servings: 5

Cooking Time: 35 Minutes

Ingredients:

- 12 dried apricot halves, quartered

- ⅔ cup whole, unsalted almonds

- ½ cup green pumpkin seeds (pepitas)

- 4 cups air-popped lightly salted popcorn

Directions:

1. Place the apricots, almonds, and pumpkin seeds in a medium bowl and toss with clean hands to evenly mix.

2. Scoop about ⅓ cup of the mixture into each of 5 containers or resealable sandwich bags. Place ¾ cup of popcorn in each of 5 separate containers or resealable bags. You will have one extra serving.

3. Mix the popcorn and the almond mixture together when it's time to eat. (The apricots make the popcorn stale quickly, which is why they're stored separately.)

4. STORAGE: Store covered containers or resealable bags at room temperature for up to 5 days.

Nutrition Info:Per Serving: Total calories: 244; Total fat: 16g; Saturated fat: 2g; Sodium: 48mg; Carbohydrates: 19g; Fiber: ; Protein: 10g

Creamy Shrimp-stuffed Portobello Mushrooms

Servings: 3

Cooking Time: 40 Minutes

Ingredients:

- 1 teaspoon olive oil, plus 2 tablespoons

- 6 portobello mushrooms, caps and stems separated and stems chopped

- 6 ounces broccoli florets, finely chopped (about 2 cups)

- 2 teaspoons chopped garlic

- 10 ounces uncooked peeled, deveined shrimp, thawed if frozen, roughly chopped

- 1 (14.5-ounce) can no-salt-added diced tomatoes

- 4 tablespoons roughly chopped fresh basil

- ½ cup mascarpone cheese

- ¼ cup panko bread crumbs

- 4 tablespoons grated Parmesan, divided

- ¼ teaspoon kosher salt

Directions:

1. Preheat the oven to 350°F. Line a sheet pan with a silicone baking mat or parchment paper.

2. Rub 1 teaspoon of oil over the bottom (stem side) of the mushroom caps and place on the lined sheet pan, stem-side up.

3. Heat the remaining 2 tablespoons of oil in a 12-inch skillet on medium-high heat. Once the oil is shimmering, add the chopped mushroom stems and broccoli, and sauté for 2 to minutes. Add the garlic and shrimp, and continue cooking for 2 more minutes.

4. Add the tomatoes, basil, mascarpone, bread crumbs, 3 tablespoons of Parmesan, and the salt. Stir to combine and turn the heat off.

5. With the mushroom cap openings facing up, mound slightly less than 1 cup of filling into each mushroom. Top each with ½ teaspoon of the remaining Parmesan cheese.

6. Bake the mushrooms for 35 minutes.

7. Place 2 mushroom caps in each of 3 containers.

8. STORAGE: Store covered containers in the refrigerator for up to 4 days.

Nutrition Info:Per Serving: Total calories: 47 Total fat: 31g; Saturated fat: 10g; Sodium: 526mg; Carbohydrates: 26g; Fiber: 7g; Protein: 26g

Rosemary Edamame, Zucchini, And Sun-dried Tomatoes With Garlic-chive Quinoa

Servings: 4

Cooking Time: 15 Minutes

Ingredients:

- FOR THE GARLIC-CHIVE QUINOA

- 1 teaspoon olive oil

- 1 teaspoon chopped garlic

- ⅔ cup quinoa

- 1⅓ cups water

- ¼ teaspoon kosher salt

- 1 (¾-ounce) package fresh chives, chopped

- FOR THE ROSEMARY EDAMAME, ZUCCHINI, AND SUN-DRIED TOMATOES

- 1 teaspoon oil from sun-dried tomato jar

- 2 medium zucchini, cut in half lengthwise and sliced into half-moons (about 3 cups)

- 1 (12-ounce) package frozen shelled edamame, thawed (2 cups)

- ½ cup julienne-sliced sun-dried tomatoes in olive oil, drained

- ¼ teaspoon dried rosemary

- ⅛ teaspoon kosher salt

Directions:

1. TO MAKE THE GARLIC-CHIVE QUINOA

2. Heat the oil over medium heat in a saucepan. Once the oil is shimmering, add the garlic and cook for 1 minute, stirring often so it doesn't burn.

3. Add the quinoa and stir a few times. Add the water and salt and turn the heat up to high. Once the water is boiling, cover the pan and turn the heat down to low. Simmer the quinoa for 15 minutes, or until the water is absorbed.

4. Stir in the chives and fluff the quinoa with a fork.

5. Place ½ cup quinoa in each of 4 containers.

6. TO MAKE THE ROSEMARY EDAMAME, ZUCCHINI, AND SUN-DRIED TOMATOES

7. Heat the oil in a 12-inch skillet over medium-high heat. Once the oil is shimmering, add the zucchini and cook for 2 minutes.

8. Add the edamame, sun-dried tomatoes, rosemary, and salt, and cook for another 6 minutes, or until the zucchini is crisp-tender.

9. Spoon 1 cup of the edamame mixture into each of the 4 quinoa containers.

10. STORAGE: Store covered containers in the refrigerator for up to 5 days.

Nutrition Info:Per Serving: Total calories: 312; Total fat: ; Saturated fat: 1g; Sodium: 389mg; Carbohydrates: 39g; Fiber: 9g; Protein: 15g

Cherry, Vanilla, And Almond Overnight Oats

Servings: 5

Cooking Time: 10 Minutes

Ingredients:

- 1⅔ cups rolled oats

- 3⅓ cups unsweetened vanilla almond milk

- 5 tablespoons plain, unsalted almond butter

- 2 teaspoons vanilla extract

- 1 tablespoon plus 2 teaspoons pure maple syrup

- 3 tablespoons chia seeds

- ½ cup plus 2 tablespoons sliced almonds

- 1⅔ cups frozen sweet cherries

Directions:

1. In a large bowl, mix the oats, almond milk, almond butter, vanilla, maple syrup, and chia seeds until well combined.

2. Spoon ¾ cup of the oat mixture into each of 5 containers.

3. Top each serving with 2 tablespoons of almonds and ⅓ cup of cherries.

4. STORAGE: Store covered containers in the refrigerator for up to 5 days. Overnight oats can be eaten cold or warmed up in the microwave.

Nutrition Info:Per Serving: Total calories: 373; Total fat: 20g; Saturated fat: 1g; Sodium: 121mg; Carbohydrates: 40g; Fiber: 11g; Protein: 13g

Rotisserie Chicken, Baby Kale, Fennel, And Green Apple Salad

Servings: 3

Cooking Time: 15 Minutes

Ingredients:

- 1 teaspoon olive oil

- 1 teaspoon chopped garlic

- ⅔ cup quinoa

- 1⅓ cups water

- 1 cooked rotisserie chicken, meat removed and shredded (about 9 ounces)

- 1 fennel bulb, core and fronds removed, thinly sliced (about 2 cups)

- 1 small green apple, julienned (about 1½ cups)

- 8 tablespoons Honey-Lemon Vinaigrette, divided

- 1 (5-ounce) package baby kale

- 6 tablespoons walnut pieces

Directions:

1. Heat the oil over medium heat in a saucepan. Once the oil is shimmering, add the garlic and cook for minute, stirring often so that it doesn't burn.

2. Add the quinoa and stir a few times. Add the water and turn the heat up to high. Once the water is boiling, cover the pan and turn the heat down to low. Simmer the quinoa for 15 minutes, or until the water is absorbed. Cool.

3. Place the chicken, fennel, apple, and cooled quinoa in a large bowl. Add 2 tablespoons of the vinaigrette to the bowl and mix to combine.

4. Divide the baby kale, chicken mixture, and walnuts among 3 containers. Pour 2 tablespoons of the remaining vinaigrette into each of 3 sauce containers.

5. STORAGE: Store covered containers in the refrigerator for up to days.

Nutrition Info:Per Serving: Total calories: 9; Total fat: 39g; Saturated fat: 6g; Sodium: 727mg; Carbohydrates: 49g; Fiber: 8g; Protein: 29g

Conclusion

Have you trained yourself to cook these treats?

You will see how healthy and good this type of nutrition is.

I'm sure your kids and the whole family loved it.

I always recommend talking to a nutritionist before starting any diet or nutritional plan.

Is your family happy? And the kids?

Follow me for more recipes.

Thank you

CPSIA information can be obtained
at www.ICGtesting.com
Printed in the USA
BVHW041359200421
605393BV00001B/364